because...

writings from a tainted life

R. K. Riley

ISBN-13: 9780692372166
ISBN-10: 0692372164

For my earth...the reason I can stand
For my sun...the reason I can see
For my stars...the reason I can hope

Contents

Forward

I had one of **those** childhoods...
and that's all you really need to know.

To Make Them Love Me

To make them love me
I would have walked a thousand miles barefoot in the snow
I would have rolled bare in hot coals

To make them love me
I would have stuck bamboo shoots under my nails
I would have pulled my hair out strand by strand
To make them love me
I would have swallowed razors, chewed glass, drank battery acid

To make them love me
I would have gouged my eyes out
I would have pierced my hands and feet with rusty nails

To make them love me
I would have gladly done all of these things
But instead

I did what was more torturous and far more deadly
I closed my eyes
I shut my mouth
I spread my legs
While they violated my body
Shattered my mind
Ripped my heart out
And decapitated my soul
I closed my eyes

I shut my mouth

I spread my legs

To make them love me

Meant

I was meant for so much more,
than being just your baby whore.
More than this half life,
not whole, filthy rotten to the core.

I was meant for so much more,
than tattered clothes and hemless lies,
echoed remnants of a prettier life.

I was meant for so much more,
than cowering, bleeding on the floor
screaming loose the consuming roar.

I was meant for so much more,
than nightmares wrenched through gritted teeth,
innocence stolen by an unmitigated thief.

I was meant for so much more,
than dancing dirty for nasty eyes,
than wishing, praying, begging to die.

I was meant for so much more,
than licking up shame after your score,
than watching my light slammed in the door.

I was meant for so much more,
than breathing death up on my knees

than listening to you plead,
please, please, please.

I was meant for so much more,
than being just your baby whore,
than ugly words tangled in ugly lies,
than drawing breath run rancid with endless cries.

I was meant for so much more,
than being just your baby whore.

I Said No

I said no
no one heard me
no one would listen
I said no
I screamed it
it echoed off the walls
endlessly reverberating
up and down the halls
bouncing off the harsh reality
and even harsher stares
of anger and disbelief
I said no
I screamed it
I begged and pleaded it
over and over
it was muffled in the pillow
drowned out by everyone's denial
unanswered by the world
I said no
I screamed it
I begged and pleaded it
I cried it out
I whispered it in their ears
as they came to take what was left
when they came to fill me with their lies
when they came

I said no

I screamed it

I begged and pleaded it

I cried it

I whispered it

I said no

no

even when I said yes

no

I said no

Hush

hush now
don't you cry
says the father to his child
his lips against hers tightly pinched
let me kiss you, open up
so I can taste the nectar of innocence
and lust
hush now
says the father to his child
reach your hand but not for mine
for that place where pleasure and power
intertwine
hush now
says the father to his child
let me cut you, down, down deep
so your blood can bloom and flow
against skin so white, new fallen
snow
hush now
says the father to his child
spread your legs, spread them wide
lie still, be quiet
let me fall into you
the healing rain of your essence
slain
hush now
says the father to his child

it's all over now, I promise

child of mine

it's over now

but that was a lie.

The Hole

there is this hole...dead center in my chest
its dark as night, wet like rain
it bleeds
and it aches
dark matter webs bleed their sickly die
from its abysmal center
leaching out in endless lace across my skin
I see it pulsing just below the white of lies
I wear for the world.
this skin so innocent..
covering,
hiding,
obscuring
the poison that runs through me,
cutting me out of this world
unfit for the next.
just pieces of a being
just pieces of rot and filth
seeping death, spurring destruction...
my vision, my sight, my heart, my life...
for good?
a mere tease...
a haughty laugh from hell
either way
gifted or black bile
alone in pieces

never whole
never real
either way
no one still

Verse and Rhyme

It's just a blank page
White on white
Space on space
It can hold anything
And everything
It already does
The possibilities in this breath
The choices I haven't made yet
The wishes I gently cry
The anguish I can only deny
It holds all
Greatness
Weakness
Strife
Illuminates this dark and ageless night
It calls to me from far behind
Singing softly of verse and rhyme
It beckons me
Again and again
To fill it up
Let the words wend
A gliding river from my soul
To reach that place among us all
On this blank page where
We can still hear heaven's call

It Doesn't Matter

It doesn't matter
It doesn't matter how many miles I run...iPod screeching in my
ears...feet burning against the pavement
    Smack
    Smack
    Smack
    Fire scorching up my shins
    Across my chest
    Jaw so tight my teeth ache
It doesn't matter
It doesn't matter how many times I say IT...how many secrets I
dredge up from the well of hell...
Burning my tongue...running acid from my eyes...leaving tattoos
of fingerprints necklacing my throat
It doesn't matter
It doesn't matter
How many nightmares I scream through...
How many sheets I piss...
How many pajamas I drench with the rankest stench of fear
It doesn't matter
It doesn't matter
IT DOESN'T MATTER
How many ways
I try to fix IT
Talk about IT
Don't talk about IT
Swallow IT down

Puke IT up

Slice IT out

Stab IT in

It doesn't matter

It NEVER

     EVER

         WILL

Because there isn't enough road to run

Because there aren't enough words to say

Because there aren't enough sheets to change

Because there aren't enough

SCREAMS, TEARS, VOMIT, and BLOOD

To UNDO a single, solitary moment of IT

To make any of it better

Because there isn't enough of ME left to save

I'm Not Yours

I'm not yours
you can't make it so
try as you might
shoving yourself in night after night
tracing your name in red against my angel skin so white
over and over
it still won't work right
what you want
what you need
isn't something you can see
        or touch
                or feel
                        or steal
it lingers deep
in a quiet, soulful place
that no violent grasping can erase
you taste it, I know,
with each insistent, relentless kiss
that burns less sweet than it once did
but it eludes you time and again
what makes me gentle
lets me win
i'm not yours
you can't make it so
you'll never taste it, hold it, know
what I would have given if freely chose
my love for you

sweet and small
presented grace, acceptance all
my heart breaks clean and true
you wouldn't,
        couldn't,
                hear me call
your name amid the raucous screams
demanding pain and penance paid
for every wound and warrant laid
i'm not yours
you can't make it so
tremble no more
let it all go
there is no more
i'm nothing left
an empty, hollow vessel bereft
no longer a prize to possess
just an ashy shadow remains
an echo lost on deaf walls
i'm not here anymore
all goodness gone
i'm not yours
you can't make it so
struggle no more
sleep, my daddy, sleep
let the angels sing you sweet and low
sleep, my daddy, sleep
please,
let me go.

i'm not yours
you can't make it so.

Instead

Beneath the blanket of evil
Among the prompters of ultimate sins
On the swamp of toxic lies
On my knees
With tears in my eyes
Under stares of hateful gaze
In the darkest ocean of sinful tides
Underneath the cloak of sadness
In the grasp of evil
       Instead of
              Beneath the lush willow tree
              Among the daisies and snapdragons
              In the grass of sweetest touch
              On my knees
              With the lady bugs
              Under the warm eyes of the sun's smile
              In worlds of adventure unknown
              Underneath the umbrella of innocence
              Beyond the grasp of evil

Come To Me

come to me
my little doll
come to me
make me real
end this swirling, raging sea of unreality
open up
my little doll
make room
let me in
so I can be
tornadoes swirl inside my chest
painful pulls to pasts and yet
if you come to me
my little doll
you can make me whole
set me free
let me fill you with this siege
so I can rest
so I can breathe
come to me
my little doll
your pain,
your damaged skin,
your warmth surrounding me
will fill my empty cavernous need
to find
a place where quiet

takes my mind

releases my blackened rage

at the lack of space, of air, of place

come to me

my little doll

let me take you to the scary place

where nothing is and I reside

deep inside you

deep inside my mind

where there is no echo

only space

come to me

my little doll

make me free

make me real

once and for all

Write, Write

I see that wall
barren and white
it begs
it pleads
it screams
write
write
write
write until the screams subside
write until the ink runs dry
write until your fingers bleed
write until you cannot see
fill it with the hate and rage
fill it like an endless page
and I think if I could write
find a pen black and thick like night
I might find that place
where quiet lives and
peace I'd find
if I could just write
see it all in black and white
then that angry blood red sight
would melt away
and make me right
would let me finally live
my life

...there

was...

no...

rest...

April 28, 2012

So, let's get semantical..(okay, yes, I am fairly sure that is not a real word)..but let's talk about some real ones. I harbor a particular loathing for certain words, some because of ridiculous over usage: i.e. love, peace, acceptable, inappropriate, forgiveness, horror...

Others I despise because I cannot even pronounce their existence, their reality into this world by the mere utterance of their syllables in proximity to each other. I try to...I try to get them to pass off my tongue as if I weren't a freak with some major (think maybe I should capitalize, underline, bold, or italicize THAT adjective?) issues...

I don't even want to write those "unmentionable" words...

If I don't say them..they aren't true

If I don't think them..they don't exist

If I don't let myself remember them..it didn't happen..

A high school geometry proof gone schizoid...

Okay, so you get where my logic train takes me, right? It's an express too – no milk train here, no stops at Normalsville or Sanitytown for this depraved freighter...talk about baggage cars...

Sorry..i digress...and occasionally regress....and often repress...

Someone shoot me now...

To get back on track here (I swear these maniacal metaphors will cease eventually...say it with me now...DEFENSES...good, good..)

Let's just take one word on my peeve list:

Ready?

Here it comes...

(two points if you can guess it right)

RECONCILE

Webster's New Pocket Dictionary (which I just nicked from my fourth-grader's backpack) says:

1. make friendly with

(save me now...we WILL be coming back to this one..bet your britches on it..)

2. settle (a quarrel)

3. to make agree or fit

4. to make acquiescent

It has been said to me that I need, should, would benefit from reconciling with my past, that it would help bridge that chasm between then and now, bad and good, etc, etc, (gag me with a spoon) etc..

So shall we take a look at what exactly that might look like:

4. to make acquiescent (pause, hold the phone, I gotta look up acquiescent now..just to be thorough)

Fuck me...

I am not making this shit up...

CONSENT WITHOUT PROTEST

So, I am supposed to consent without protest to the things that happened to me, with me, in me, outta me, as a child.

Pause.

Let that sink DEEP into the gray matter.

Didn't I already DO that – oh, I don't know, like a THOUSAND times? I closed my eyes, I spread my legs, I didn't scream...what more could you want in a victim, right?

Pretty sure THAT would be the epitome of consent without protest.

MOVING ON –

3. to make agree or fit

Can I make myself agree with what happened to me as a child?
Hell, I can't even acknowledge (another word peeve for another
rant) that it happened at all most of the time. Can I make my
experiences of "unmentionables" fit with my world view? No. Can
I make them fit with my current life? Um, again, No. Can I make
them fit with anything I can understand..make sense of
...tolerate...No. Nada. Nay...sayeth the woman.

Onward and upward (up yours seems to fit better...get it?...fit?...I
really am unwell, aren't i?)

2. settle (a quarrel)

Well, quarrelling was definitely involved..fairly one-sided
though..especially since I consented without protest but one can
only spread one's legs so far, you know...so my failings in my
ability to stretch myself like Elastogirl may have been construed
as arguing...who knows really what crazed and depraved baby
rapists construe as quarrelling..their versions of consent are
certainly suspect...

Anyways...

Settle..rings of make peace with...make even steven...settle a
debt...decide who is right..who wins...

No contest.

All consent.

No protest.

They win.

Done.

Settled.

And the piece d'resistance...

My personal favorite...

1. make friendly with

To quote my four-year-old...

"Seerriously, Mommy?"

Make friendly with..as if the unmentionables were a rude, spiteful new kid at school, or a feral cat, or broccoli...

     Seriously?

          Really?

You wouldn't ask a young woman who lost her father in 9/11 to become BFF's with an Al-Qaeda extremist??

You wouldn't ask the mother whose child was killed by a drunk driver to have him over for tea and stale cookies?

But me—

reconcile

     make peace

          and the penultimate platitude of perversity...

               ACCEPT...

..what was done..

Did I mention that it's unmentionable??

Make friendly with it..

Settle it...

Make it fit...

Agree with it...

Fucking just

CONSENT WITHOUT PROTEST

Look me in the eye and tell me to do that.

Look me in the eye and tell me to consent without protest.

One more time.

It's for my own good, right?

It's the only way to heal and move forward, right?

Look me in the eye and tell me to spread my legs..bend
over..consent...one more time?

Don't you see?

It's already done.

      I already reconciled.

          I closed my eyes.

             I spread my legs

                and didn't say a

                single,

                solitary,

                unmentionable

                word.

Cross Your Fingers

I cross my fingers
and close my eyes
please, please not tonight
school was hard
my head aches
my friends were mean
the jungle gym ripped my jeans
I cross my fingers
and close my eyes
please, please not tonight
my stomach hurts
everyone's home
my sheets are clean
any chance you won't be mean?
I cross my fingers
and close my eyes
please, please not tonight
I don't want to
there goes the door
creaking feet across the floor
I can't do it
not tonight
my body hurts
it isn't right
I cross my fingers
and close my eyes
please, please not tonight

but you are here
breath hot with want
reaching for what was mine
but hasn't been for decade's time
I cross my fingers
and close my eyes
please, please not tonight
the pain screams through
drips down the walls
the sheets are ruined
you've taken it all
nothing left but a bloody core
of a little girl no more
I cross my fingers
and close my eyes
please, please let me die tonight

this girl ain't gonna run

you'll have to come at me with more than a slap,
more than an evil jeer
you'll have to come at me with more than a fight,
more than a dirty kiss
because this girl ain't gonna live like this
because for the first time I can see it from the other side
where light shines bright and every move is right

you'll have to come at me with more than needles and pins
you'll have to come at me with more than anger and rage that
never wins
you'll have to come at me with more than a hand to make me
black and blue
because this girl ain't gonna move
because for the first time I can see it from the other side
where the light shines bright and every move is right

you'll have to come at me with more than a knife,
more than a gun
you'll have to come at me with more than a frightful death
because this girl ain't gonna run
because for the first time I can see it from the other side
where the light shines bright and every move is right

Even Though

even though I know the truth
that lust and lies smile out behind all eyes
I still stand up
hold my head up just so high
to catch a whisper of the sun's rise
and even though I have watched
my innocence splatter across their feet
seeping between the dainty cracks along the floor
I have to believe that there is more
more than just this vile hate
that consumes
and waits
and waits
and waits
until my head lolls gently right
and my breath stretches a bit less tight
it is then
with swiftness sure
their rage can no longer bear endure
my hair tangles tight
my head snaps back
with every resounding, deafening crack
of all those fragile, magic walls
that I have built since oh, so small
to keep out monster's darkness might
to hide, reflect, shine out only light
but they have waited

patient

sure

for one more chance to kiss the pure

the sweet

the meek

that which was once so out of reach

I lay here waiting

watching the broken pieces

silently fall

come

come one

come all

the feast will begin

it won't be long

just hold your breath

it's almost dawn

the sun will break

dance off my lips

they have waited an eternity

for this

There Isn't Much To Say

There isn't much to say
except that I can't see your face
your eyes that hold only the light of perfect love, amazing grace,
the song of doves.

There isn't much to say
except I can find no other way
to reach for you in this hellish place where endless screams howl
and ache.

There isn't much to say
except we knew this time would come
where hope and faith would finally come to die.

There isn't much to say
except I am sad to see me go
I had begun to believe I might perhaps get free.

Wicked Confection

you were not the only one to kiss my name in scarlet blood
dried and caked
between knuckles raw
from breaking
bending
every law
your hands were not the first
nor last
to grasp and grab
that filthy
fetid
trash
that left you grimy
soiled
pleasured
raw and real
panting gruesome want
revealed
I didn't blame you
not now
not then
my wicked confection
your virtue's
end

When I Was Perfect

I was perfect
lily white
skin so soft it felt like breath
eyes that had never seen darkness
a heart open, encompassing the universe
all of heaven's love
radiating
illuminating
I was perfect
and you ruined me
you painted my luminous skin
      with blood
            with hate
                  with your sickness
you made me drink you darkness, consume your lust, swallow
your lies
you cut my skin with needles and knives
delved into my gentleness with pins and parts
      poking
            burning
                  torturing my perfect space
turning it into hell
my perfect innocence
      blackened and burned
      tattooed forever with your evil ink
you sewed my eyes shut

erased my voice

        left me naked in the cold

I was perfect

and now I'm dead

nothing but a vessel, a broken shell, an empty chalice that once

held

everlasting life

     perfect

         endless

             limitless

               timeless

now running over with come and blood

tears and flesh

I was perfect

and you ruined me

I'm left to hold it all

to try to make a life from degradation, shit and shame

left to find a way to hold it all in, crush it all down, push it all

away

so that I can breathe

now I'm left

ruined

imperfect

trying to find a way out

trying to find a way to wash myself white

back to soft angelic skin

eyes gleaming with innocent love

heart so full it eclipses the sun

now I'm left

---

trying to find my way back

to before

to before you ruined me

back to when I was perfect

Swaying in the Light

I stand here swaying
the stars fall from heaven
like rain
I stand here swaying
as they illuminate the pain
and wash it quietly from my dirty skin
I stand here swaying
as the wind whispers
through my hair
each breeze a kiss of tender rest
I stand here swaying
swaying in the light
I stand here swaying
making love to the night

If only

if only it hadn't happened
if only I could hold it long enough to feel its truth
but the glimmers dance quickly across my eyes
a blur of ifs ands whens
and wonders why
it couldn't have been
it mustn't be
it isn't real
no matter how much I see
or feel
or taste
or hear
my name...over and over...
come here
come here
the weight of hands against my throat
upon my chest
not the worst by any measure yet
it cannot be
it shouldn't be
how can I know?
how can I see?
that grotesque visage unraveling me
in silent jest...it jeers and sweetly whispers
you know it's true
so true

my dear

everything you see

and feel

and think

oh no, it couldn't have been

every nightmare, flash, and scream

all are true and then

those unseen

those you run from, my dear, oh dear

they will find you

as will he

never fear

you tell yourself no, no

he's gone

dead and buried

long lost to the dawn

but you know better

deep, deep down there

you know he was just

here

where he will always

always

be

so run all you want

deny

hide

die inside

the worst is yet to be

True Way

I play in darkness
fake in light
my true face disintegrates
upon illumination's gaze
the black veil of my true way
wends and binds
between my legs
a feline curl of evil whispers
snakes inside that place
where midnight rules
this vacuous space
and haunted howls
screech unheard
against sooted windows
rotted nailed
holding unsteady up to
the interloping world
threatening dominion
over shameful sovereignty
in my kingdom's rule
of lie and touch moves
enters this abandoned cradle
for desire's sake and
abysmal need
to feel and move
all is greed

and I am left

no inside still

no substance

no ability to move

within these damp and dreary

insipid walls

no sovereignty

no face

at all

Break Me

break me
break me until the sun won't shine
break me until the tears run dry
break me with the blinding shame
break me until I forget my name
break me until the moon screams red
break me until your need is fed
break me mourning
break me night
leave no hole, no crack, no light
break me jagged
break me smooth
sing me lullabies of nothing true
break me open
break me right
turn my world
only hell bent night
break me ugly
break me true
leave me empty
lay me cruel
break me last
break me fast
let me die
this endless past

...I

never...

caught...

my...

breath...

because…

Amazing…really…this ridiculous notebook. It's been buried in my closet for almost 5 years judging by the poetry..pre-death and pre-baby…poems, notes, whispers of ideas mixed amongst baby accessory lists and Christmas budget lists from 2007.
But that is exactly, perfectly, the point, isn't it?
My childhood clashing endlessly with my present…a flying roach caught in a glass canning jar, wings beating ceaselessly against the armor of my mundane, jeans-and-t-shirts, suburban domesticity and while that characterization is hardly doing justice to my beautiful, real, quiet family life, it does highlight the radical shift from one end of life's possibilities to the other. That shift..that dizzying gradient often leaves me wandering endlessly through a narrow shaft, a deep gully, that culvert in between.
I would imagine it's a bit (or maybe a lot) like what immigrants from horribly destitute third world countries experience upon reaching our fat and self-satisfied geography. More dog food in one aisle of our local grocery store that they ate all the previous year.
For me, it's school lunches with multi-colored cupcake cozies so those glorious sugar creations replete with coordinating sprinkles arrive pristine to my starving school children, only to be eaten way before the all-natural homemade cola jerky or the organic, sea salt potato crisps. And it's bake sales, scrapbooking nights, endless cookbook reading and even more endless cleaning, shopping, loving, bandaging, friending, supporting, educating, caring, laundering…whew..you get the idea. Delicious, devilish domesticity…

Except,

    except,

        I have my own dog food aisle...
That long row, carefully lit with pulsing fluorescent lights that
leave no shadows, only stark true-to-life color reality...
my dog food aisle, a truly horrific, unbearably ugly childhood,
teen hood, and bits of adulthood thrown in for good measure...
and in between the cakes mixes and that pesky jar of pimentos I
can never seem to find...there a memory will sit, all trimmed out
in day-glo colors that ad exec's swear have the capacity to suck
consumer's hands directly to the box and promptly into their
cart. There it sits..a day-glo memory...no coupon needed, no
special pricing..though occasionally they are buy one get one
free...and no matter how many times I walk past it...ignore
it..face it..hell, even embrace it..it still stays there...waiting for
the next time I come in searching for those infernal pimentos.
So, you are probably asking by now, R.K., what exactly is the big
deal here? The memories are there. You know they are. Why not
just make peace with it...why not just let it go already?
The answer, my dear reader, is...
Because

    Because

        Because this isn't a fight with a boss..this isn't an
ugly divorce..or a car accident or a singular rape or, well,
anything else (except for those things which ARE worse, and,
yes, there are many but those folks would get it, would
understand "BECAUSE").

This is something that no matter HOW many times I look at it, IT never changes. IT never EVER isn't IT. It is always what it was and it will never, can never, be okay or made peace with...are you fucking kidding me with that bullshit?? It will always be what it is...when someone can come along and make it NOT what it is then I will consider revising my view. But I'm pretty sure that would involve airborne pigs or some serious LSD usage or the return of the Messiah...

not going to hold my breath...

instead, I'm going to push my crappy, crooked, squeaky grocery cart straight past that screaming, bleeding, violent memory..I'm going to leave it lying on that shelf and maybe, just maybe when I'm four aisles away gently lowering that tiny jar of pimentos into my cart,

I might,

   just maybe might,

     be able to stop

       crying.

Lies

It was a lie.
All of it.
Every single, solitary second of it
was a lie.
A lie you told yourselves and
tried to heave on me.
It was a lie.
That's why it never satisfied.
It's why you had to tell it
over
and over
and over
again
in so many ways
with such rage and vengeance.
It was a lie.
Repetition didn't make it true.
Force didn't make true.
Brainwashing didn't make it true.
A thousand times and thousand times didn't make it true.
It was a lie.
You couldn't make yourself real by annihilating me.
What is true...
What is real...
You annihilated yourself
over
and over

and over

again

with vengeance, force, and rage.

It was all for you.

Not me.

You punished, beat, attacked

yourself.

And you got what you deserved.

Not me.

You got a violent

endless reminder

of your non-existence.

Every time you violated me

you sent yourself further into that pit of hell

where you can't feel or breathe.

It was a lie.

A lie you told yourself.

It was what you needed me to believe.

I don't.

I don't believe you.

It was a lie.

Do you know how I know?

Do you?

Because I AM still here.

Feeling, thinking, breathing,

and you are still where you have always been

are who you have always been

nowhere

and

no
one.
It was a lie.

All Done

my head is heavy
my eyes on fire
my back is screaming
i'm all done in
i don't have anything left to give
my teeth are grinding
my jaws clenched
my hair is brittle
i'm all done in
i don't have anything left to give
my feet are bloody
my fingers raw
my nails shattered
i'm all done in
i don't have anything left to give
no breath
no voice
no strength
no life
i'm all done in
i don't have anything left to give
what held me up
is broken and worn
what kept me moving
is run dry and torn
i'm all done in
i don't have anything left to give

except a sigh

a dry kiss

a dying, battered wish

Limited Reality

limited reality
the gray, empty space between then
and forever
it is where many of us live out our existence
it is the space between
the guardians of what has been and
the watchers of what will be
limited reality
this chair
this room
this night
this place
limited in size, texture, color
limited reality
the bonds of the here, of the now
the shackles of our narrow awareness
our blind locomotion
to a distant point that fades as we laboriously approach
it is our myopic sense of time and
place and
space
inner and outer
it is the confinement of our essence
the funhouse mirror distortion
of our glorious beauty
it is the jumbled chaos of the notes of
our harmony

blared at deafening volumes in our ears

limited reality

the tenacious tentacles of disbelief in what

could

might

is

should

be

it is our limited reality

that concrete, single-minded,

caging fixation on only what is

solid

present

tangible

proven

limited reality

that which damns our souls to

boredom

isolation

disease

starvation

leaving only ghostly echoes in the night

shadows on the wall

it is our limited reality that

jails us

torments us

haunts us

it is our limited reality

that

kills

us

Nothing

the world can scream its never-ending wail of agony
bellow its unechoing keening over the emptiness of
its lost
ancient
light
it can scramble and rage against the
dense
defiling
void
where majestic love once stood
it can grasp at shadows ceaselessly
filling its vacuous lungs with the
poisonous
sinuous
whine of empty belonging
to a mirage of false and sinewy traitors
but it all falls deaf
at my white feet
only silence's gentle lullaby kisses at my ears
the world's lustful
greedy
depraved
desires nothing but soft sand beneath my feet
as I wander slowly
purposefully
gently to the horizon's light
gently to you

the world in all its blackened lies must fall before me

broken at its knees

for I hear nothing

not even a whisper of its evil

it must bend and break before me

for I hear nothing

am nothing

but the rocking song of your grace

"Forgiveness is the fragrance that the violet sheds on the heel
that has crushed it."
Author Unknown

A beautiful, an achingly beautiful statement..
I try to imagine, sometimes, what it would be like to forgive
them..to wrap them in the same radiant, complete, whole,
glorious light and love I feel for my children, my husband, my
friends, and sometimes, complete strangers.
Anyone who has spent any real time with me knows where I can
allow myself to go into compassion for another...vivid imagination
married to slightly above normal sensitivity leading to full
hearted empathy.
But violet–laced forgiveness?
The idea of it is intriguing..
What character, what compassion would it take for me to see
them in such a way as to allow me to let go of the injury, the
righteous anger and indignation?
Could I let myself go there, fully, completely, centered in my
fledgling faith in the laws of a compassionate, perfect universe?
Could I see them in all their sickness..could I see them with the
eyes of God?
Or maybe it's the crushed part of this haunting description that
appeals to me...
Did I leave them with the sweet, gentle fragrance of innocence?
Could they smell my soul on their hands, clothes, on their skin?
Could they taste that perfect, fresh, virginal kiss long after I was
gone?

Is that why they kept coming back? Searching for that first,
heavenly time when I was clean and fresh and perfect?
What did I taste like to them?
Cotton candy, lemon drops, caramel ice cream, sun-warm
strawberries, the first snowflake melting on the tongue, a single
tear on a baby soft cheek?
What did I smell like to them?
Summer rain on spring flowers, the wind, wood smoke and pine,
juicy lush peaches?
I want to believe I smelled of those things.
I want to believe I tasted of those things.
But that part of me, that dark, crushed part of me
             knows that I didn't
             knows that I don't
I taste of sickness, rotting, decaying road kill gore.
I smell of putrid, fetid, depraved need.
I taste of lies, shame, blood, and cruelty...
        sawdust, sweat, rage, and lust...
But I didn't always...
        once
             a very, very, very
                  long time ago...
I smelled like heaven
and I tasted like God.

Need

They had a pressing need...
so they turned me inside out.
Snatched me by my hair
and a single SNAP of the wicked wrist
and there I was
inside out
showing the world every inch of my private, tiny insides.
They had a burning need...
so they turned me inside out.
And now my clothes don't fit right,
my shoes squish and slurp when I walk....
my hairbrush snarls on knots of sinew where it once slid with
ballerina grace
along shiny, unstained locks...
no point brushing my teeth, only gums and tissue flapping in the
breeze.
They had a desperate need...
so they turned me inside out.
I can't see a dang thing,
just an achy, inky blackness that kisses wet against my eyelids....
my hands don't work,
keep grasping only to find empty throbbing space
that smears fire across my fingertips and trails ashes down my
wrists...
I can't hear,
no voices, no music, no laughter, no wind,
only a warbled, tinny moan from my ocean echo of hell

when I tilt my head just so.

They had an undeniable need...

so they turned me inside out.

So all I can be is a naked, broken body...

so all I can do is drag myself damaged through the world....

so all I can have is a wasted and worn existence...

because all I can see

        and taste

           and smell

              and feel

                and hear

is their

pressing

burning

desperate

undeniable

need

    for me.

It's like a dark ocean of water pulling me down, warm and wet, wrapping itself around me like an ebony shroud, hooded and soft. The waves churn and rumble below me, calling my name so quietly, so smoothly, like satin against a perfect painted night sky. I've been under for so long, sometimes briefly breaking the onyx surface just long enough to feel the sun, the sting of salt in my eyes, seeing all those I love on the beach so white and blinding. But they are so very far away and the water is so warm, so achingly beautiful in its quiet, ceaseless humming against my ravaged skin. My legs are so weary from fighting against the current and my heart beats wildly against my chest. My breath so ragged and uneven but I hear them...my babies...calling out to me. Their voices singing with the wind. I want so much to reach them, hold their warm cheeks against my cold, wet skin...smell their hair and that place in their necks where I can taste infinity...but the water is so strong...

I know I see things others don't. I feel things differently than most. The hardness of the desk right now...the gentle curve of the keys as I type...the quiet vibration of the air around me disturbed only by the movement of my chest and my fingers on the keys...and sometimes I can be mesmerized by the exactness of things...the solidity of reality...

...but there is another reality...less solid...less mesmerizing...and it rips at my core...trying to eat me alive...those shadows behind people's eyes, the lazy curl of ink beneath their skin...the crude and ugly scars that no one else can see that rip across their countenance, distorting their masks...revealing the evil only I can see.

People watch horror movies as entertainment, happily munching their popcorn and candy, laughing at the grotesque imitation of fear and murder and blood and death. They have never seen it staring back at them in the mirror...someone unrecognizable underneath the layers of blood and skin, matted hair and dried come. They've never watched their skin split open...never lingered for what seems like years as the blood slowly reaches the breech and spills over on the bed sheets, blooming petals of hell against the rainbows and unicorns. No horror movie could ever, ever come close to that. And when it does...I've watched their eyes divert to their popcorn buckets...seen them nervously sip their sodas...hoping desperately to avoid that sinking feeling in their stomachs...that gentle nudge of sickness that makes it all too real for them...because the moment has gotten too close...not to something they have experienced but to their deepest fear of the reality, the solidity of evil...and they can't watch, can't imagine. Because on screen there is no smell, no wetness, no warmth. The sounds are muted by bad music and the angles shift but that isn't how it really is. The angles don't shift. He is always right there in front. The smells are overpowering, burning the nostrils with their acrid, dense, putrid stench and the scenes don't end minutes after they have begun. They go on and on for hours, weeks, days, and years, replayed over and over...not in reruns on HBO but in the head, in the night, in every fucking goddamn breath....

...maybe I am cracking up, maybe this is the beginning of my madness...always, in every moment, seeing that there is no chasm between the light and the dark...no space between the evil and the perfect...in me they lay together...naked...intertwined like webs...the screaming and the lullabies.

Sunday Mornings...

It's Sunday morning, sun bounces off the stained glass resting
against the frigid window.
I have just enough time to wonder what time it is when...
Swoosh goes the door
And the padding of bare five-year-old feet thump, thump gently
against the carpet.
He's on the bed as quick as I can blink the last kiss of sleep
away.
Little, thick hands, his daddy's hands, squish my cheeks as he
plants a good morning mama kiss on my nose.
He tumbles over me, grasps the half of the pillow I have offered.
Snuggling under the quilt, he sandwiches my hand between his.
"I like our hands like this, Mommy."
His perfect skin glows against the pressing dawn.
His lashes so long I can hardly believe they are real.
"Mommy, you are the bestest mommy I ever had."
His little bow of a mouth, so beautiful it makes me almost believe
in god.
He kisses me again, full on the lips, closes his eyes and sighs
deeper into the pillow.
Bliss.
Another Sunday morning, sun bounces off the rainbow sun
catcher hanging against my bedroom window.
I have just enough time to consider if I can change the sheets
and what is left of my pajamas before someone comes in when
The floor in the hall creaks...
The hinges of my door answer back.

And the heavy thumps of giant feet lurch across the carpeted floor.
He's on the bed as quick as it takes me to blink back that lone tear threatening to fall from my eye.
Big, thick, angry hands, my daddy's hands, rub against my cheeks,
A good morning daddy kiss against my neck.
He tumbles over me, grabs at my long hair, pulling in a deep, shuddery breath I know all too well.
He shoves off the quilt, sandwiches his hand between my legs.
"I like you all warm like this, just waiting for me."
His dark eyes sucking every bit of light out of the dawn, his teeth so sharp I can hardly believe they are real.
"My nasty little thing...tightest piece ever."
His cracked lips sneer as he growls against my chest, so horrible, so ugly, I can't believe in god.
"Fuck me baby girl."
He kisses me again, full on the lips, closes his eyes, and sighs into me even deeper.
Hell.

Reality Violence

everyone thinks violence is loud
like on tv or in movies
tables crashing as limp bodies are flung with ridiculous ease
through the air
hands punch and connect
against a jaw
KABLAM
CRACK
SMACK
like cannons
like bombs
glass shattering
10 on the Richter scale
Rock 'em sock 'em
Violence
Violence..real...honest-to-god violence
isn't like that
Violence, real violence,
can be
often is
wish it wasn't
quiet
clumsy
disgusting
ugly
it isn't choreographed

music tracked
            perfectly timed
it is real
      no noise
            no music
                  no steps
it's his hand punching your face
the only sound...a dull thud as your head bounces off the wall
and the only fading edges aren't around the scene
just your vision
your mouth still tastes like the bologna with mustard sandwich
you were eating
with just a hint of copper penny from the hole you bit in your
tongue as your head hit the wall
The dogs are still barking outside
just like they were before you FUCKED UP and flinched away
from his hand reaching up your shorts under the table
      Damn
      Two for flinching
      One punch, one pinch
Right THERE, between, where he was aiming with that wayward
hand
Your mother is still chewing her tuna on rye
didn't miss a bite
Violence is quiet
it is clumsy
he has mustard on his hand from your lip
Violence is real
it is disgusting in its ability to fit itself in anywhere

ANYWHERE

ANYTIME

WITHOUT A SOUND

so quiet

The smack of his lips as he licks the neon drop off his knuckle

The swoosh of your napkin across your bleeding lip

The squeak of your chair across the floor as you try to move just
a bit away

longer reach

Violence is quiet

> clumsy

>> disgusting

>>> ugly

Violence is quiet

but if you listen

Very

Very

Very

carefully

underneath the dogs barking, the people chewing, the chair
squeaking, the napkin swooshing, his hand rubbing

you can hear it

maybe

shhhh

Can you hear that?

the clumsy, disgusting, ugly quiet of it??

that unending...deafening...

ROAR

A thousand waves

chasing a thousand tornadoes
racing after a thousand bombs
that
      THAT
             is
                   me
                        screaming

...because

...their

evil...

never...

slept.

The Dark Side of Me

I have this place—in the very back of my head...no, it's not that mythical "happy place" I've heard tell of, nor is it the "happy place" my Pilates instructor (read fresh, downright dewy faced demon bound in spandex and a ponytail) tells us to go to before nailing us with scaled 100's (if you don't know what that is, considered yourself blessed).
No, the place out back...I slide there quiet like, smooth as my royal icing on a sugar cookie...quiet...no one even knows I've gone.
And if I could take you with me, you, the casual observer, would be hard pressed to see the differences.
Maybe that's why it feels less like a disassociation than just a subtle shift in the gradient of my reality...a hue change...just a bit more red than before...just two clicks right of center...five minutes later on the sundial...the shadows slide just a bit farther across the floor...
To you it would be the same
but to me
those ever so subtle differences
they are
everything.
They are the only reason I am still alive.
So let's take a peek...a quick spin inside my slightly–less-than-sane snow globe...no hints though...think of it as a "What's Wrong In This Picture" from the Highlights from Hell magazine.

My house...this room...my beloved bedroom..gorgeous with its deep chocolates, caramels and ebony...the kids smiling, stunning faces in the photos that still take my breath away and blatantly refuse to give it back..

The bookcase overrun and faintly sagging to the right, not unlike, ironically, my mother-in-law...all my rocks on the windowsill, anchoring me to my dear friendships, guarding against the phantom evil night dwellers that dangle outside my window...

The stained glass, found on clearance at Target, eons ago, bouncing light and color...my lover's socks tangled in a crazy knot on the floor, defying physics and most positions in the Kama Sutra...

I kick them in the closet as I have every night for nearly twenty years...

my bed..ancient, soft, where I hope to be allowed to pass my last breath...

and where I am fairly certain a hot wheel car is currently under my bum...

the beaded charms hanging willy-nilly from the lighted garland above my bed...good dream charms from my child...that the wiley one guaranteed would stop me from screaming in the middle of the night if he put them there...never argue with a ten-year-old red head...they are wicked clever and just a wee bit dodgey.

My whole life is in this room, this house, this family.

And the only way I know to stand up tall in it

is to slide

to slide backwards into this parallel world

where every exterior thing is exactly as it is in reality

everything down to the hot wheel leaving a bumper imprint on
my tush
everything is exactly right
everything
except
me.
When I slide back those imperceptible, minute, whispers of
change happen...
Scars are erased from my skin like dried glue peeling from a
preschooler's hands.
My jaw loosens as the chains that clamp it shut recede, clickety
clacking back behind my shoulder blades.
With each sweet, easy breath, my lungs expand past the ugly
girdles that hinge them small.
I can feel my feet and hands, my legs and torso..that hot hell
hole between my shoulders cools, quietly drifts off in easy waves,
leaving the salty brine of the sea tickling my nose.
The giant bomb-punched chasm at the center of my chest fills in
like diamond shimmer sand cascading into an hourglass.
The ever-always-never-not-present groping ghosts cease their
incessant, slimy clawing across my body
And the rank aftertaste of shame and terror slides back down my
throat and my mouth is flooded with the taste of rainbow
sherbet.
and that scream
that oh my god scream
that no scream
that no more
please

god

no

more

scream

sings itself a lullaby, snuggles deeper into the pillow and goes to sleep.

I know this place in the back of my head isn't real.

I know it's just a symptom (sigh)

         An adaptation (uggh)

         A fucking craziness (ahhh, yeah, baby)

I know it isn't real.

But the alternative

to see it as it is

to be me in all this beauty

     in all this innocence

        in all this safety...

It would paint it every horrifying shade of hell the likes of which Home Depot never dreamed.

It would fill its every corner and closet and drawer with blinding pain and grimy wicked lust.

It would leave a stench that no cookies baking or steaks grilling or bleach bleaching could dispel.

It would break every mirror; rip apart every neat and tidy seam.

It would turn every beautiful family picture into porn.

And make every single spoken word a keening, wailing scream.

It would turn it all ugly,

       bloody,

          horrifying,

            and ruined.

It would turn it
into
me.

<u>Prick</u>

prick. prick. prick. prick. prick. prick. prick. prick. prick. **10**.

prick. prick. prick. prick. prick. prick. prick. prick. prick. prick.

prick. prick. prick. prick. **25.** prick. prick. prick. prick. prick.

prick. prick. prick. prick. prick. prick. prick. prick. **39**. prick.

prick. prick. prick. prick. prick. prick. prick. prick. prick.

prick. prick. prick. **54.** prick. prick. prick. prick. prick. prick.

prick. prick. prick. prick. prick. prick. prick. prick. **69**. prick.

prick. prick. prick. prick. prick. prick. prick. prick. prick.

prick. **82.** prick. prick. prick. prick. prick. prick. prick. prick.

prick. **92**. STOP. Admit it...you stopped actually reading the word

a while back...prick. prick. prick. prick. I don't blame you. I did

too. prick. prick. **99**...but every time that hypo needle would

pierce my skin...prick. prick. prick. prick. prick. prick. **106**...down

there...in there...prick. prick. prick. prick. I would jump, just a tiny

bit, but that tiny bit...prick. prick. prick...would earn me another

one...so I tried to count...prick...to be still...prick...still as

stone...prick...and finally...he stopped...prick....can you count them

all...each and every   single   solitary   painful   jab...I did... I had

no choice....it was that or die....prick....all **118** of them....

No Solace

There is no solace
I keep seeing that book,
all dog-eared, well-handled, yellowed pages curling in on
themselves as if they
need to hold their secrets in just a bit.
Not me.
I hold mine in a lot,
so tight each step I take twangs like an old guitar, taut with age
and disuse.
That book...
passed, I'm sure, from hands to hands
        patient to patient
                loved one to loved one.
Tears have wet the pages, anger seeping in the smiling white
gaps between the
words.
People see themselves there,
        their stories similar, and different...
Pains, sorrows, fears, rages, dreams, and nightmares...and above
all, experiences,
experiences...
gently, lovingly, sung chapter after chapter.
A perfect harmony of resonate experiences.
We, nodding gently, rhythmically,
We know you have been hurt,
                abused,
                        mistreated.

We, leaning just slightly closer, quieter even,

We know you are damaged,

                        frightened,

                                worn.

We, reaching ever so slowly for your hand or knee,

We know how to help,

                        ease your suffering,

                                comfort your aches,

                                        heal your shattered spirit.

Yes, yes, we know...

        find solace in our solidarity,

                in our knowledge,

                        in our togetherness through the tears.

STOP!

STOP IT!

STOP IT RIGHT NOW!

Am I in that book?

Am I?

Really?

Bit and pieces...maybe...and that's a big...BIG...maybe....

Am I?

Uh-uh.

No way.

You know it.

And I know it.

There is no togetherness through the tears.

There is no comfort in the crying.

There is no solace in the suffering.

There is NO SOLACE.

Not in those pages.

Not in those four walls.

Not in someone's words

      or arms

            or life.

There is no solace.

I can give you a hundred reasons why.

Tell you a hundred stories to prove it.

Show you a dozen scars to make it screamingly real.

But it wouldn't matter...

It would still just be me...

Standing alone,

in the corner,

blood pouring from the holes in my mouth,

bands dangling from my burned wrists,

screams long worn too thin for even god to hear.

But it wouldn't matter..

There is no solace...

Not then...

Not now...

Not ever...

Night

if only to catch a glimmer of the moonlight
in hopes of finding peace this night
for I search so long, so far
to find thee in this dark
to know thy presence
strong and true
to mend the aches of ashes soon
my heart longs repentance nil
I find thee absent, absent still
the moonlight shines so jagged bright
but there is no end to this long night
a mere reflection of the truth
this orb does mock my longing sight
for I have glimpsed the endless light
shining high, shining right
warmth's embrace dangled close
a breath on my cheek
a whisper at most
the stars do not speak or sing
only blink as if unseen
by these wanting eyes
mocking me on this long night
for no peace, nor rest will alight
upon my lashed eyes tonight

In Desperation

In desperation, we will cheat.
We will lie.
We will steal.

In desperation, we will run.
We will fight.
We will fly.

In desperation, we will hunt.
We will climb.
We will survive.

In desperation, we will hit.
We will rape.
We will kill.
We will save.

In desperation, we will torture.
We will sacrifice.
We will go insane.

In desperation, we will plead.
We will beg.
We will weep.
We will rage.

In desperation, we will endure.

We will recover.
We will triumph.

In desperation, we will change.

Starlight Bright

a ray shimmer gold from eyes of innocence
a touch of simple pleasures twinkle on cheeks of youth
a warming spirit speaks gentle to the mind
on hair of golden blossoms
the embrace of light leaves streaks
that glow even through dark of night
covered by a cloak of sorrow
the light still grasps on
to hold her soul
in its rainbow embrace
under wings of heaven light
a child sleeps
in starlight bright

They filled me up when I was but so little...filled me up before my sunshine was ripe...before my heart got its wings on straight and could fly right...before my eyes had decided, for sure and for certain, what color they were...before my hair got straightened out and knew which way was down...

They filled me up so very full with their sad, sad stories and short, short breaths that all the sunshine got squeezed right out through my poor upside down eyes who couldn't navigate at all what with the confusion...and my pretty heart wings broke all off in tiny bits as they tried to fly away and now they sulk in a scratchy nest in the back of my throat.

They filled me up so very full when I was so very little that I'm all outta room in here and I can't even sit down what with all their junk about. I think I would very much like to be a little less full now. Maybe just a smidge of space, here or there, my left pinky finger perhaps...or just there behind my right eye...so I might, maybe might, get to glimpse a bit of smile or foolish wishing now and then.

Not much space at all, really, I'm small and don't need much air...just a tiny, clean square somewhere with just enough room that I may shuffle my feet when the wind sings at night or stretch my arms a little ways, not too far, when the sun begs for a bit of verse and rhyme.

I am small and don't need much, I'm hardly anyone at all.

But they filled me up so very much when I was oh so very small.

About the Author

R. K. Riley lives in the Midwest with her husband and three children. This is her debut poetry collection.

rkrileywrites@gmail.com

www.ingramcontent.com/pod-product-compliance
Lightning Source LLC
Chambersburg PA
CBHW051734040426

42447CB00008B/1136

* 9 7 8 0 6 9 2 3 7 2 1 6 6 *